Leap Out

Advisory Panel
Sharon Adams
Marilyn Bailey
Susan Davis
Sue Evans
Demetra Georgopoulos
Vangie Kalanderopoulos
Nancy Leonard
Linda Miller
Miriam Trehearne

Senior Program Consultant
Jennette MacKenzie

Program Consultant
Christine Finochio

I(T)P Nelson

an International Thomson Publishing company

Toronto • Albany • Bonn • Boston • Cincinnati • Detroit • London • Madrid • Melbourne
Mexico City • New York • Pacific Grove • Paris • San Francisco • Singapore • Tokyo • Washington

I (T) P® International Thomson Publishing

The ITP logo is a trademark under licence
www.thomson.com

© Copyright 1999 ITP®Nelson

Published by

I (T) P® Nelson

A division of Thomson Canada Limited
1120 Birchmount Road
Scarborough, Ontario M1K 5G4
www.nelson.com

Printed and bound in Canada
2 3 4 5 6 7 8 9 0/ML/7 6 5 4 3 2 1 0 9

Canadian Cataloguing in Publication Data

Main entry under title:

Nelson language arts

Contents: (v.1) Step out – (v.2) Reach out – (v.3) Leap out
ISBN 0-17-618557-7 (v.1) ISBN 0-17-618558-5 (v.2) ISBN 0-17-618559-3 (v.3)

1. Readers (Primary). I. Title: Nelson language arts 2.

PE1119.N443 1998   428.6   C98-932551-2

Executive Editor: Susan Green
Project Editor: Anne-Marie Wallace
Production Coordinator: Theresa Thomas
Art Direction and Design: Liz Harasymczuk
Permissions: Jill Young
Equity Consultant: Ken Ramphal

Table of Contents

Unit 1: Getting Together

Children everywhere share the same kinds of experiences and dreams. In this unit you will read:

- stories
- poems
- personal wishes

BE A BETTER READER

- think about what you know
- learn the parts of a story
- predict what will happen in the story by looking at the pictures

Whoa!

Written by Sheree Fitch
Illustrated by Joe Weissmann

NO!
squabbling
or
nibbling
no
scratching
or
clawing
no calling
me names
that bite
i
n
t
o
my
heart

YES!
listening
yes
sharing
yes
nuzzling
yes
caring
just loving me
right from
the start

Mama, Do You Love Me?

Written by Barbara M. Joosse
Illustrated by Barbara Lavallee

Mama, do you love me?
Yes I do, Dear One.
How much?

I love you more than the raven loves
his treasure,
more than the dog loves his tail,
more than the whale loves his spout.

How long?

I'll love you until the umiak flies
into the darkness,
till the stars turn to fish in the sky,
and the puffin howls at the moon.

Mama, what if I carried our eggs—
our ptarmigan eggs!—
and I tried to be careful,
and I tried to walk slowly,
but I fell and the eggs broke?

Then I would be sorry.
But still, I would love you.

What if I put salmon in your parka,
ermine in your mittens,
and lemmings in your mukluks?

Then I would be angry.

What if I threw
water at our lamp?

Then, Dear One,
I would be very
angry.
But still, I would
love you.

What if I ran away?

Then I would be worried.

What if I stayed away and sang with
the wolves and slept in a cave?

Then, Dear One, I would be very sad.
But still, I would love you.

What if I turned into a musk-ox?

Then I would be surprised.

What if I turned into a walrus?

Then I would be surprised and a
little scared.

What if I turned into a polar bear,
and I was the meanest bear you ever
saw and I had sharp, shiny teeth,
and I chased you into your tent
and you cried?

Then I would be very surprised
and very scared.

But still, inside the bear,
you would be you,
and I would still love you.

I will love you,
forever and for always,
because you are my Dear One.

AFTER YOU READ

Write about a picture

Choose a picture you like. List the things
you learned about the story from looking at
the picture.

Left Behind

Written by Carol Carrick
Illustrated by Donald Carrick

READING TIP

Use pictures to predict

Before you read, look at the pictures. Make a chart like this one. Write what you think will happen in the story.

What I Think Will Happen	What Really Happened

Christopher was excited when his class got on the bus to the city. Instead of going to school that day, they were going to the aquarium. He thought the best part would be when the bus dropped them off so they could ride on a subway.

Mrs. Snow was the leader of this group. She counted them before they went downstairs to the train. "Does everyone have a partner?" she asked.

Christopher grabbed Gray's hand. "I've got one."

Downstairs, Mrs. Snow put a token in the turn-stile as each of them went through. Christopher could hardly wait for the train to come. He had never been in the subway before. Why was it taking so long? Then from far down the track they heard a rumble. Headlights shone in the dark tunnel.

"It's coming," shouted the children.

The train roared into the station. It was so loud that Christopher held his hands over his ears.

As soon as the doors slid open, he started into the first car.

"Wait, wait!" said Mrs. Snow. "We all get on together."

Everyone took a partner's hand and climbed on.

"Can we look out the front of the car?" asked Christopher.

Mrs. Snow nodded. "But be sure to hold on."

The doors closed and the train moved out of the station into darkness.

Christopher and Gray pressed against the window, watching the signal lights change from red to green. The car rocked back and forth as they moved faster and faster. The brakes squealed around a sharp curve.

"Whoa!" Christopher yelled and he grabbed for a pole.

"Hold on," called Mrs. Snow.

When they got off the train, Mrs. Snow counted them again. "Take your partner's hand. Let's stay together," she said.

The aquarium was in a large building next to the harbour. While their teacher was buying tickets, Christopher peeked in at the big fish tank.

"Look," he said, running past the windows. "Turtles."

"Let's not get too far ahead, Christopher," Mrs. Snow called.

The class moved slowly from window to window, looking at big fish and little ones. But it was hard for Christopher to stay back with Gray; he was so excited.

Then it was time to go home. Christopher wanted to stand in the front of the first car again, but the train was too crowded. So he held onto a pole by the door.

Every time the train stopped, people pushed out and more people pushed on. Soon he was surrounded by strangers. He couldn't see anyone from his class, not even Gray.

The next time the train stopped, a crowd was waiting to get on. Behind Christopher, people were shoving toward the door.

"Let them off," someone called.

Christopher and the people around him stepped down onto the platform to let the others off.

The crowd on the platform pushed onto the train. Just as Christopher was about to get back on, a man squeezed in ahead of him. Before Christopher knew what was happening, the doors closed and the train was moving.

"Wait!"

Christopher started running, bumping into people along the platform. "Let me back on," he called, but the train didn't stop. Helplessly, he watched it disappear into the tunnel.

Christopher looked wildly around the platform. All he saw were strangers. How was he going to get home?

Another train came, and he panicked. Should he get on? He didn't know where it was going. He read the signs but none of them meant anything to him.

Christopher knew he had to get someone's help, so he went upstairs to find a police officer. He searched the station from one end to the other without seeing one. The smell of a doughnut stand was making him hungry. He looked in his pockets, but he didn't have enough money.

Maybe Mrs. Snow would come back for him. He'd better wait where he had gotten off so she could find him. Christopher went downstairs. Was this the same platform? Now he was all mixed up. If only he had stayed with Gray; then he wouldn't be alone now. He tried hard not to cry.

A man in uniform came up to him. "What's the matter, kid?" he asked. "Are you lost?"

"I got off and the rest of them didn't," Christopher said.

"Do you know where you're supposed to be going?" Christopher shook his head no.

The man talked to someone on his radio, and in a few minutes a police officer came. People stared as he wrote down Christopher's name and where he lived.

"How did you get lost?" the police officer wanted to know.

Christopher explained.

"Are you taking me home?" he asked.

The police officer said something he couldn't hear because another train was coming. Then they went to a waiting room in a different part of the station.

"Sit here," the police officer said.

"How will my teacher know where I am?"
Christopher asked.

"We'll radio a call to every station. When we
find her, we'll bring her here."

Christopher sat while the police officer talked to
a man at the desk. He wondered how long it would
be till the class noticed he was gone. He kept
watching the clock on the wall. It seemed to take
forever. Would Mrs. Snow be angry? And what
about the other kids? He wiggled on the hard chair.
They would think he was dumb.

After a long time he heard footsteps. "Mrs. Snow!"

She was coming down the hall with a police officer. Christopher jumped off his chair and ran to her. He was glad to see her even if she might be angry.

"I was scared you'd never find me," he said.

Mrs. Snow looked relieved. "I was scared, too."

They said goodbye to the police officer and went out on the platform. A train was going by. Christopher thought the people in the windows looked like fish in a tank.

"Everyone is waiting on the bus for us," said Mrs. Snow.

When their train came, Christopher was happy to take her hand and get on it.

AFTER YOU READ

Check what really happened

Look back at your chart and fill in what really happened in the story. Did the pictures help you predict what the story would be about?

Ladder to the Sky

Written by Sheree Fitch
Illustrated by Kevin Hawkes

READING TIP

Make mind pictures

Authors make pictures with words. As you read these poems, use the authors' words to make pictures in your mind.

Do you know
If you try
You really can
Touch the sky?

Lean a ladder
Against the moon
And climb, climb high
Talk to the stars
And leave your handprints
All across the sky

Jump on a cloud
And spend the day
Trampoline-jumping
Through the air
Climb a rainbow
And watch the world
From way up there

Then ride that rainbow slide
Back home.

Running

Written by Nikki Grimes

When I run,
I don't have to think
about home or school.
There're no rules
to memorize,
or break, or keep.
I don't have to compete
or try to beat anybody
to prove a point.
All I have to do
is take a deep breath
and go.
I don't even
have to know
how fast
I fly.

New World

Written and illustrated by Shel Silverstein

Upside-down trees swingin' free,
Busses float and buildings dangle:
Now and then it's nice to see
The world—from a different angle.

AFTER YOU READ

Use describing words

Choose one of the poems and draw a mind picture
you saw as you read the poem. Around this picture
write the describing words the author used.

The Crane Girl

Written and illustrated by Veronika Martenova Charles

Yoshiko lived with her parents in a village by the
sea. In the mornings she went for walks with her
mother and found pretty pebbles on the beach.

In the evenings she played with her father when
he returned home from fishing. Soon there would
be someone else to play with. Yoshiko's mother was
going to have a baby.

28

It was exciting when the new baby arrived. He was tiny and soft and smelled like morning after the rain. Yoshiko's father named him Katsumi and everybody loved him.

But now there were fewer walks with mother. All day long she was bathing and feeding the baby. Now there was not as much playing with father. He wanted to play with Katsumi too. Yoshiko began to think her parents no longer loved her.

The day her parents gave Katsumi his omamori amulet to protect him, Yoshiko was jealous. It was made from the same cloth and had the same designs as the omamori they had given her. Now she was certain she wasn't special any more.

Yoshiko became more and more unhappy. She wanted to be a baby again. She was sure her parents wouldn't even notice if she went away. So, Yoshiko walked through the misty morning toward the sea.

At the beach, she saw fish playing in the rippling water. *Pishan, pishan*, the fish splashed.

"Could I be one of you?" Yoshiko asked them. "Then I could be your baby and bathe with you. Then I would be happy." But the fish didn't answer, so she walked further.

In the forest, she saw monkeys swinging in the sunlit branches. *Kii, kii,* the monkeys chattered.

"Could I be one of you?" Yoshiko asked them. "Then I could be your baby and eat nuts with you. Then I would be happy." But the monkeys didn't answer, so she walked further.

On the hilltop, she saw a flock of dancing cranes. *Cur-lew, cur-lew,* the cranes cried.

"Could I be one of you?" Yoshiko asked them. "Then I could be your baby and dance with you. Then I would be happy." But Yoshiko was so tired from walking that before the cranes could answer, she fell asleep in the tall, cool grass.

The cranes took pity on her, for she was such a lonely child.

"So be it!" said the leader. And together they swooped and whirled around her in a magical moonlit dance.

When Yoshiko awoke the next morning, she was a baby crane. All that remained of her human life was the omamori amulet her parents had placed around her neck for luck.

The cranes treated her like one of their own. They took her for walks and played with her and fed her mayflies with their beaks. As she grew older, they taught her how it was to fly, and they taught her to dance.

Yoshiko stayed with the cranes and the seasons passed. But whenever she soared over the village by the sea, she remembered her family and wondered how they were.

Then one day, Yoshiko decided to find out. She flew to her parents' house and perched high on a tree in the garden. There, she overheard her mother and father telling a sad story to Katsumi.

It was about their precious first-born child; their beloved daughter Yoshiko, and how they missed her. Katsumi sighed and wished he had a sister to play with.

When Yoshiko saw how much her parents worried and how Katsumi needed a playmate, she wanted to be a girl again.

Cur-lew, cur-lew, she called, but they didn't understand. She leapt into the air and swooped to the ground. She bowed and stretched her wings.

She began to dance to show them she was well, but still, they didn't recognize her. Tears sprang to her eyes. She whirled round and round until she was dizzy.

She jumped so high that she caught her wing on a branch and tore it badly. Then, hurt and exhausted, Yoshiko fainted and crumpled to the ground.

When Yoshiko opened her eyes, her family was leaning over her. Katsumi fanned her with a branch. Her mother tended the wounded wing while her father dripped cool water into her beak. Happiness filled her heart. For the first time in a long while, Yoshiko felt truly loved again.

As her mother gently stroked Yoshiko's feathers, her fingers closed around something familiar. A look of wonder appeared on her face. It was Yoshiko's omamori!

"Yoshiko?" she whispered.

At the sound of her name the magic of the cranes ended, and Yoshiko became a girl again. Her parents were overjoyed to have her home and she finally understood they had never stopped loving her.

In the days that followed, Yoshiko heard the cranes calling, *cur-lew, cur-lew*. And when she did, she would touch her omamori and remember how it was to fly.

Then she and Katsumi would dance together under the sky, to show the cranes she was happy.

AFTER YOU READ

Make a list

Write three new words you learned in the story. How did you figure out what they mean?

My Wish for Tomorrow

READING TIP

Think about what you know

Do you have a wish for the future? As you read, think about what that wish would be.

I wish that people did not make fun of other people.
—*Stephanie Sotiris, Age 7, England*

I wish for my friend to get better, for the weather to be good, to have clean water, and for everybody to be well.
—*Pandora Bilali, Age 6, Greece*

Wish: That young people
wouldn't forget old people.
—*Renato Reyes, Age 4, Peru*

To have peace and health and trees for oxygen.
—*Vicky Theodorou, Age 7, Greece*

Do not trash the forest.
—*Bryce Alexander Marshall, Age 6, Australia*

My wish is to make a big flying carpet so that
I can fly on it around the world to make friends.
—*Sonali Handalage, Age 8, Sri Lanka*

I wish everyone would be
friends—nobody was ever sad
and nobody ever felt left out in
games and in the spring and
summer months many fields
were filled with sweet smelling
flowers and the world was
allright and safe. That's how I
wish the world to be.
—*Rachel Tsang, Age 9, China*

I wish the world would be happy forever after.
—*Dumolone Dube, Age 6, Zimbabwe*

AFTER YOU READ

Write a wish

Write a wish you would have for tomorrow and draw a picture to go with it.

A Salmon for Simon

Written by Betty Waterton
Illustrated by Ann Blades

READING TIP

Learn the parts of the story

A good story has a beginning, a middle, and an end.
As you read, think about the parts of this story.

All summer Simon had been fishing for a salmon.
"It's the king of the fishes," he told his sisters.
"We know," they said. "That's why great-grandmother calls it Sukai."
When Simon was little, his sisters had taught him how to catch minnows with a strainer. But this year his father had given him a fishing pole of his own, and he had been fishing every day.

42

He hadn't caught a single salmon.

Now it was September. It was the time of year when many salmon were swimming past the island where Simon lived, near the West Coast of Canada. They were returning from the sea, looking for the rivers and streams where they had been born. There they would lay their eggs so that more salmon could be born.

One day, when the tide was on its way out, Simon and his sisters went clam-digging. When their pail was full, his sisters took the clams home to their mother to cook for supper, but Simon stayed on the beach. He had his fishing pole with him, as he had every day that summer.

"I'm going to stay and fish for salmon," he said. And he did.

He sat on a rock and fished.

He sat on a dock and fished.

But he didn't even see a salmon.

He saw red and purple starfish sticking to the rocks.

He saw small green crabs scuttling among the seaweed.

He saw flat white sand dollars lying on the wet sand.

He saw pink sea anemones waving, pale jellyfish floating, and shiners swimming.

But he didn't see a salmon.

"Are they ever hard to catch," thought Simon. He decided to stop fishing, maybe forever.

Simon walked back along the beach to the place where he and his sisters had been clam-digging. The sea water had oozed up from the bottom of the hole and filled it. Some seagulls sat beside it. When Simon came near, they flew up into the air, crying, "*Keer, Keer, Keer.*"

"I'm not good at catching salmon, but I am a good clam-digger," thought Simon.

He dug a few clams and put them on a nearby rock. The gulls flew down, picked up the clams in their beaks, carried them into the air and then dropped them. The clams hit the rocks, and the shells broke open.

Simon listened to the *bang, bang, pop* as they shattered. He watched the gulls fly down and eat the soft clam meat.

Then Simon heard something different, something that sounded like *flap, flap, flap.*

"What's that?" he cried, but nobody answered.

He heard it again—*flap, flap, flap*—and this time the sound was right above his head.

"*Keer, keer,*" shrieked the seagulls, flying off. Simon looked up, and there, not very high above him, was an eagle. Its strong black wings beat the air as it climbed toward the treetops.

Simon had often seen bald eagles, but this one was different, for it was carrying something in its talons—something that glistened.

"A fish!" cried Simon. "He's got a fish!"

He was so excited that he began hopping about and flapping his arms like eagle wings. The seagulls were excited, too, and they circled overhead, screeching.

In all the stir and confusion, the eagle dropped the fish. Down it came out of the sky...
down...
down...
down...
SPLAAT...SPLASH
into the clam hole!

The fish lay on its side in the shallow water and did not move.

Simon ran over. "It's dead," he cried.

But just then the fish flicked its tail and flipped over. Its gills opened and closed, and its fins began to move slowly.

"It's alive," shouted Simon. Then he looked closer. His eyes grew round. "It's alive and it's a *salmon*. This must be the most beautiful fish in the whole world," he thought.

For it was a coho, or silver salmon, that had come from far out in the Pacific Ocean to find the stream where it had been born. It had grown big in the ocean, and strong.

All summer Simon had been waiting to catch just such a fish, and here was one right in front of him. Yet he didn't feel happy.

He watched the big handsome fish pushing its nose against the gravelly sides of the clam hole, trying to find a way out, and he felt sorry for it. He knew it would die if it didn't have enough water to swim in.

Simon wanted the salmon to be safe in the sea where it could swim and leap and dive. He didn't know how he was going to save the salmon, but he had to find a way.

"I won't let you die, Sukai," said Simon.

Simon thought of carrying the fish to the sea, but he knew it was too big and heavy and too slippery for him to pick up.

He thought about waiting for the tide to come in, but he knew the salmon couldn't wait that long.

He looked up at the circling seagulls, but all they said was "*Keer, keer.*"

Then, as he looked around, Simon noticed his clam shovel. An idea popped into his head.

He would dig a channel for the salmon to swim down to the sea. That was what he had to do.

Simon began to dig. The wet sand was heavy. He dug and dug.

After a while he stopped and looked to see how far he had gone, but he had not gone very far at all. He kept on digging.

His mother called him for supper, but he couldn't go because he hadn't finished yet.

The salmon was lying quietly now in the shallow water, waiting.

The sun dipped low in the sky, and the air became cool. Simon's hands were red and he was getting a blister, but he kept on digging.

At last, just when he thought he couldn't lift another shovelful of sand, he looked up and there he was, at the sea.

The channel was finished.

Cold sea water flowed into the pool. When the salmon felt the freshness of the sea, it began to move again. Its nose found the opening to Simon's channel and slowly, slowly the salmon began to swim down it.

Down, down the channel it swam.

At last it reached the open sea.

The salmon dived deep into the cool water, and then, gleaming in the last rays of the setting sun, it suddenly gave a great leap into the air.

And it seemed to Simon that the salmon flicked its tail, as if to say thank you, before it disappeared beneath the waves.

"Goodbye, Sukai," called Simon.

The salmon was free at last.

Soon it would be in the deep, secret places of the sea.

Now the sun had set and a chilly wind was starting to blow. Simon's hands were sore, and his feet were cold, but he felt warm inside. He picked up his fishing pole and his shovel and started for home.

He knew that his house would be bright and cheery inside, because lamplight shone golden through the windows.

And he knew that it would be nice and warm, because he could see smoke curling out of the chimney.

And he knew that something good was cooking for supper, because he could smell a delicious smell.

And Simon thought, as he opened the door, that maybe he would go fishing again tomorrow, after all.

But not for salmon.

AFTER YOU READ

Make a chart

Make a chart to show what happened in the different parts of the story.

What Happened in the Story		
Beginning	**Middle**	**End**

Getting Together

You have read about how people care about each other and the world we live in. Think about what you would do to make the world a better place. Work with a group and share your ideas. Then write a group list to share with others.

Think about working in a group.
What does it look like?
What does it sound like?

Plan

- Make your own list of what you would do to make the world a better place.
- Bring your list to the group.

Remember:

▶ Everyone in the group shares their lists.
▶ Look for ideas that are the same.
▶ Look for ideas that are different.
▶ Decide what to write.

Write the list

Check

Check your list for spelling and punctuation.

Check your group work

Ask:
- How well did we work together?
- Did we talk about our ideas?
- Did everyone have a chance to do something?

Here is what one group wrote.

> ## Our Wish for Tomorrow
>
> No fighting or war.
> People would be kind to each other.
> People would be kind to all living things.

Share

Post your lists in your school and share them with other classes.

Unit 2: Media Talks

You can find out information using different media. Books, television, video, newspapers, and CD-ROMs are just some of the media you can use. In this unit you will read about a group of students who use different media to find out answers to questions.

BE A BETTER READER

- use text features
- read for main ideas
- think about what you know

Information Detectives

Written by Susan Green

READING TIP

Use text features

Pictures, speech balloons, and colour boxes are called *text features*. Before you read, look at the text features to find out what the selection is about.

When you do a project, there are different ways to find out information. These children are finding out about children in other parts of Canada.

A CD-ROM is in parts like a book. Instead of finding the chapter and turning to the right page, you can find the topic you want, click on it with your mouse, and the information will come onto your computer screen.

I'll use this CD-ROM. I can find out what St. John's is like. It will give me information about how big it is, what the weather is like. I can find out almost anything.

I found a video about Canada in the school library. It should have information about Ottawa.

Videos are a good source of information. Some videos are about real places and people. They show what a place is really like—what it looks like and what it sounds like.

I'll use the Internet to find answers to the questions. I just have to type in "Winnipeg" and click on GO, and the information will come on the screen.

The Internet is called "the information highway" because of all the things you can find out when you use it. You can type in place names, people's names, and things that interest you. Information will come to you from all over the world!

I'll go to the library and look for books and magazines about Vancouver. I can check the card catalogue or use the computer to find the subject I want. The librarian can help me too.

Libraries are places to find all kinds of information. You can check the Table of Contents of books you choose to make sure they will have the information you need.

After the children did their research, they came back together to check that they had found the answers to their questions. Here are some examples of what their notes looked like.

What is the weather like in Vancouver?
- It rains a lot.
- temperature is very mild in the city
- there's snow in the mountains all year!

Ottawa

	CD-ROM	Book	Video
What would we see if we went there?	-Parliament buildings -changing of guards	-museums -mounted police -Parliament Hill	-Royal Canadian Mint -Hull -Parliament -winterlude
What do the children like to do?	-skate on the Rideau Canal -go to a ~~~	-biking -winter festival	-go to parks -go shopping at Mall
What is the weath like?			

Recipe card

Chart

What could I do in Winnipeg?

- watch coins being made at the Royal Canadian Mint

- look at polar bears and other animals at the Assiniboine Park Zoo

- watch the Winnipeg Blue Bombers play football

- see the stars at the Planetarium

- go to Winnipeg's International Children's Festival

67

Computer print-out

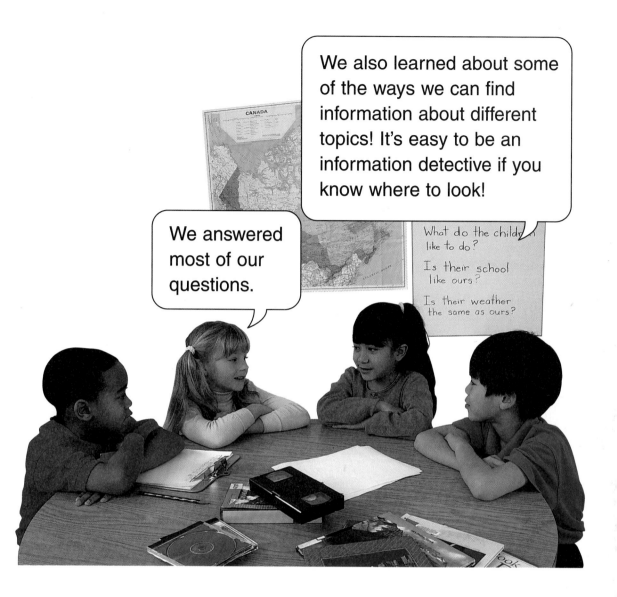

AFTER YOU READ

Make a list

What text features did you see? Pick one text feature and tell how it helped you understand what "Information Detectives" was about.

Media Talks

You have read about using media to find answers to questions about other places in Canada. If someone wanted to learn about where you live, how could you use media to answer their questions? Make your own media presentation to tell others about where you live.

Plan

You can make a storyboard to show three or four things you'd like to share about where you live.

Here is the storyboard Aileen made.

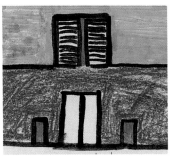
Museum

Playground

My House

Write a script

Write what you'd like to tell someone about each frame of your storyboard. This is your script.

Revise

Practise reading your script
to a partner.
Have your partner tell you:
- what they liked
- what could be better

Did I use describing words?
Did I give enough details?
Should anything be added?

> Museum
>
> This is a museum in our city.
>
> You can find out about people
> who lived a long time ago.
>
> A guide will take you on a
> tour.

Here is part of Aileen's script.

Check

Ask yourself:
- Did I use a loud voice?
- Did I talk slowly?
- Did my voice sound interesting?

Keep the video
and tape
presentations in
the school library
for others to view
and listen to.

Share

Make your presentation to the class
or put it on video and send it to someone
else you know in another part of Canada.

Unit 3: Look Closer

When you look closer at what's around you, you can learn new things. In this unit you will read:

- a "how-to" text
- an information text
- an experiment
- a story

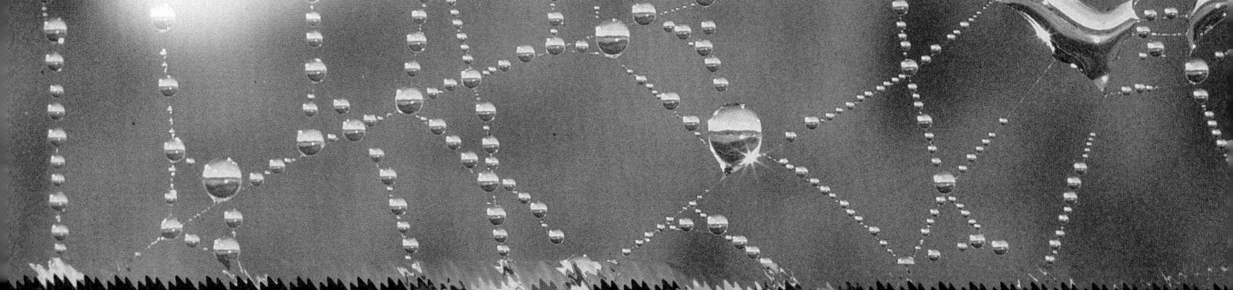

BE A BETTER READER

- ask questions
- use order and action words
- think like an author

Water, Water Everywhere

Written by Melvin and Gilda Berger
Illustrated by Bart Vallecoccia

Turn on the faucet.
Out flows the water.
Drop after drop after drop.
You fill a glass.
And take a drink.
The water tastes good.

water cycle

Here's a surprise.
The water is not new!
It has been on the earth forever.
If we are careful, there will always be plenty of fresh, clean water.

But where does the water come from?

Each drop of water is on a never-ending journey.
This journey is called the **water cycle**.
The water cycle gives us the water that we need.

Most water on the earth is in the oceans.
The oceans are salty.
The sun shines on the salty oceans.
It warms the water.

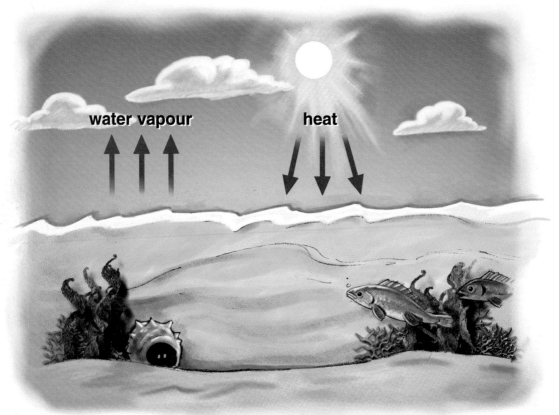

The warmth makes tiny bits of water called
molecules (MOL-uh-kyools).
The salty bits are left behind.
The water molecules form a gas.

The gas is like an invisible cloud.
It is called **water vapour**.

You can't see the water vapour.
You can't smell it.
You can't feel it.
But water vapour is in the air.
When water becomes water vapour, we say it
evaporates (e-VAP-uh-rates).

Water evaporates all
around you.
Look for puddles after
a rain.
The next day the
puddles are gone.

Wash the chalkboard.
In a few minutes the
board is dry.
The water has
evaporated.

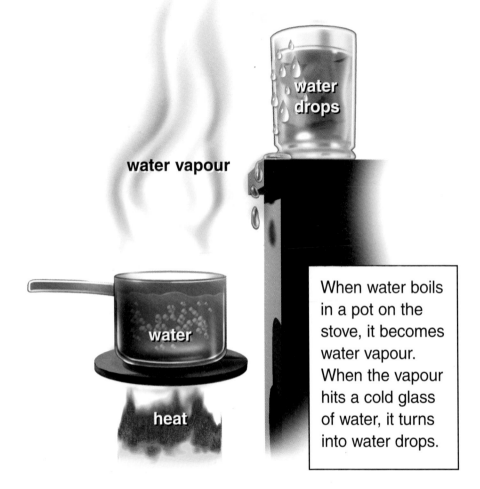

water vapour

water drops

water

heat

When water boils in a pot on the stove, it becomes water vapour. When the vapour hits a cold glass of water, it turns into water drops.

Winds lift the water vapour.
They carry it high up in the air.

Here the air is cold.
The cold air chills the water vapour.
It changes into tiny drops of water.
When water vapour becomes water drops, we say it
condenses (kon-DEN-ses).

Water vapour condenses all around you.
Breathe out on a cold day.
The cold air chills your warm breath.
The water vapour in your breath turns into a cloud
of water drops.

Take a hot bath.
The warm water causes water vapour, or steam, to
form in the air.
The water vapour condenses on the cool bathroom
mirror.

You fill a glass of milk.
The milk makes the glass cold.
The water vapour in the air
condenses on the outside of
the cold glass.

cloud

Up in the sky, billions of tiny water drops come together.
They form a **cloud**.

The drops in the cloud bump into each other.
They stick together.
The water drops grow bigger and bigger until they are so heavy they fall from the cloud as rain.

Rain, snow, sleet, and hail.
They are all forms of water.
They
   – fall from the sky
   – mostly drop into oceans, lakes, and rivers
   – evaporate from the earth
   – condense in the air
   – and fall from the sky all over again!

Round and round the water goes.
This is the water cycle.
It gives us the water we need.

AFTER YOU READ

Think about your learning

Look at the diagrams. What made them easy to read? How did they help you understand the information?

How to Make a Water Magnifier

Written by Carol Gold
Illustrated by Blanche Sims

Did you ever wish you could see a ladybug smile?
You can, if you put some water in front of your eyes.

What you need

- a small clear plastic container with a tight-fitting
  lid. The container should be round for all or most
  of its length. (Some containers that work well are
  pill vials, or film canisters.)
- a pitcher of water

What to do

1. Put the container on a table and carefully pour water into it until it's full to the very top.

2. Gently add a few more drops of water.

3. Put the top on the container. Try not to spill any of the water. If you find a bubble in the bottle, try adding more water to make the bubble as small as possible.

4. Put the top on tightly.

Now you have a marvellous magnifier!

A magnifier makes things look bigger. You can use it when you want to look at things that are too small to see clearly.

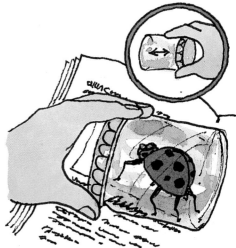

- Hold your magnifier so you can see through the water.

- Lay your magnifier sideways on the page over a drawing of a ladybug. Look through the magnifier.

You can use your magnifier to look at small things around your house and outside.

- Look at a picture in a newspaper.
- Read the writing on a penny.
- Magnify some sand.
- Take a close-up peek at a dandelion.

Your marvelous magnifier is a water lens. You can see a lot of small things through it.

Wouldn't it be nice if you could wear water drops in front of your eyes to see better?

In a way, some people do. Look at a pair of reading glasses. Their lenses are shaped a lot like large water drops.

There are lots more experiments you can do with your water magnifier. Make magnifiers out of different-sized containers and find out if they magnify differently. See what happens if you leave a big bubble in your container and look through it.

And if anyone asks what you're doing, tell them you're having BIG fun!

The Penny Experiment

Adapted from Experiment with Water
written by Bryan Murphy

Try a simple experiment to find out more about water.

- Fill a glass to the brim with water.
- Guess how many pennies you can put in the glass before the water overflows.
- Put in pennies one at a time.

Something very strange happens to the surface of water. You have to look very closely to see it.

You might think nothing else will fit in the glass without causing the water to spill over. But you can add a number of pennies before the water spills! How many—5, 10, 20, 40?

Look closely at the surface of the water as you add the pennies. The water seems to be held in by an invisible skin. This force that holds the surface of water together is called **surface tension**.

Did you know?

Some water insects use surface tension to walk on water. Other, such as this Backswimmer, swim just on or under the surface.

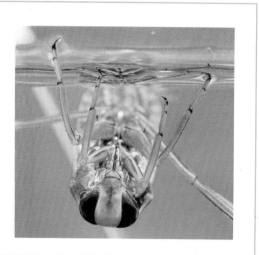

AFTER YOU READ

Make a list

Make a list of the action words that helped you read the directions. What other things did the authors do to help you read the directions?

Washing the Willow Tree Loon

Written by Jacqueline Briggs Martin
Illustrated by Stephen Marchesi

READING TIP

Think like an author

Some authors put real information in the stories they write. As you read, look for information the author puts in the story.

One fall night a barge hit a bridge and spilled a rushing stream of oil into Turtle Bay. Many diving birds—the loons and diving ducks—dived into the oily stream and were covered with oil. Many swimming and floating birds swam through the oily stream and were covered with oil.

The loon that stayed by the fallen willow tree was covered with oil. Her feathers, which had kept out water better than any raincoat, were matted and sticky and too heavy to help her fly. She shivered, swam to the shallows by the bend in the road, and began to use her bill to clean her feathers.

In the morning the first person who saw the loon drove on past. "What's one bird? It's not my worry," she said. "The world is full of birds, and I have work to do."

In the afternoon a housepainter with a long-handled net came to net the bird. His grandfather had taught him how to be quiet around birds. Others had shown him how to catch oiled birds.

But the loon was frightened and dived into the water—out of reach of the long-handled net.

The painter picked up another bird, one that had died from the oil. He put the bird into a bag, so it could be studied, and so no other animal would eat the bird and get sick from the oil.

The housepainter waited to see the loon again but did not find her. He walked on to look for other birds.

"This place has many birds," he said. "And I have work to do."

In the evening the loon went back to the shallows by the bend in the road and slept.

In the early morning a woman in tall fishing boots walked through the shallow water. Quietly, quietly, she came to the loon and netted her. She owned a bakeshop but made no cakes when there were birds to be cleaned. "Bird work is thanks for the songs I hear when I am baking in the early morning," she said.

The baker and a friend took the bird out of the net, gently wrapped a towel around her body, and carried the loon to empty boxes on a waiting truck.

The baker checked to be sure the box had air holes. She put a soft cloth on the bottom of the box for the loon to rest on, then placed the loon inside the box, inside the warm truck.

"The day is full of shivering birds," she said. "And I have work to do."

The truck took the willow tree loon and the other rescued birds—the ducks, the geese, and the herons—to an old school building where there were trained workers to help them.

A barber with gentle hands used a cotton swab to wipe the oil from the loon's mouth and breathing holes. Carefully he washed the loon's eyes with clean, warm water.

He said, "I will see the world in birds' eyes today. I have work to do." And he went to pick up another bird.

An animal doctor felt the loon for broken bones and fed her water and medicine through a tube into her stomach. The medicine would help the loon get over the oil she had taken in while cleaning her wings. The doctor had tried to mend the broken robins' wings when she was young. But the robins had always died. Now she knew what to do. She put the bird in a quiet pen to rest from the scare of many hands and strange sounds. "This place is noisy with people who all have work to do," said the doctor.

Late that night a young man came to the
schoolhouse and took the loon from the pen where
she was resting. He once had a pet duck named
Ralph. He called all the birds Ralph, and he
whispered songs to them while he poured warm,
soapy water over their feathers.

Two others helped him hold the loon in the
washtub and keep her calm. He rubbed her feathers
gently to clean away the oil. When the water was
dirty with oil they moved the loon to another tub
full of fresh water. The young man used cloth and
swabs to clean away the oil. "Three tubs of water
to clean this bird," he said. "I have work to do."

At the rinsing tub was an old woman who still kept the empty shell of a hummingbird egg she had found fifty years ago. "It's no bigger than a bean," she said. "But it started me out with birds." She had a lifetime of bird stories. Neighbours who wanted to see hummingbirds came to her house.

She rinsed the loon four times, gently spraying until plump drops of water looked like beads on the bird's back. Two others helped her hold the bird and keep her calm. Then they dried the loon with towels and put her in a pen with pillows and heat lamps. "This is your world for now. And you have work to do," the woman said. The loon began to preen her feathers.

Later, the old woman carried the bird to a deep pool, where she could swim, dive, eat, and preen. The old woman came back many times and watched until the willow tree loon was swimming easily and her feathers were as good as a new raincoat.

An artist who painted pictures of birds came in the early morning. He left his easel and his paints when it was time to set the birds free. He placed a towel over the loon and put her in a box.

He drove to a place where the water was clean. He knew that the loon could not walk on the shore. So he waded out until the water reached his knees, opened the box, and gently tipped it. He watched as the loon righted herself and swam away.

That night, the baker, the young man, the barber, the housepainter, the doctor, the woman who loved hummingbirds, the artist, and all the helpers listened for the loon.

Who knows who has heard or seen the willow tree loon since then. Maybe me, maybe you. The world is full of birds. And we have work to do.

AFTER YOU READ

Think about your learning

Write three facts you learned by reading the story.

Look Closer

You have read how to make a water magnifier and how to do a water experiment. Now write your own information text. Choose something you do everyday and write a "how-to" text that tells someone else how to do it.

Plan

Make a web that shows what you know about "how-to" text.

Ideas

- making a sandwich
- brushing your teeth
- walking the dog

Write your "how-to" text

Revise

Read your "how-to" text to a partner and have them follow your directions. Is there anything you should change? Are your directions easy to understand?

Check

Check your work for spelling and grammar. Does it look like "how-to" text?

Here is Meaghan's "how-to" text.

How to brush your teeth.
1. Find your toothbrush.
2. Wet your toothbrush.
3. Squeeze toothpaste on your toothbrush.
4. Brush your teeth up and down, left and right.
5. Rinse your mouth with water.
6. Rinse your toothbrush.
7. Put the cap on the toothpaste.
8. Put your toothbrush and toothpaste away.

Share

Make a class book of "How-Tos" and keep it at the Reading Centre.

Unit 4: Stories Alive

What makes a good story? You might say interesting characters and story problems are important. A good story also needs an author who writes in an interesting way. In this unit, you will read:

- a legend
- a fairy tale
- a chain story

BE A BETTER READER

- use different ways to figure out new words

- think about what you know

- learn about different kinds of stories

END

105

Nanabosho
How the Turtle Got Its Shell

Written by Joe McLellan
Illustrated by Rhian Brynjolson

READING TIP

Read a legend

Legends are stories that have been told for many years. As you read, think about why people tell this kind of story.

This weekend we went to the city with ni mishomis and nokomis. We went to visit our Auntie Matrine.

Auntie took us all out to a large shopping mall. While we were there, we went into a pet store to look at the animals.

"Ni mishomis," said Nonie excitedly, "look, they have turtles here. I don't know if I like that."

"Yes," said ni mishomis, "turtles belong in lakes and rivers, not in stores. Kitchie Manitou did not create turtles to be owned."

On our way back to Auntie Matrine's house, ni mishomis told us a turtle story.

■ ■ ■

A long time ago, Turtle didn't have a shell. He was a small, little green creature who spent most of his time hiding in caves.

or in trees

or under rocks for protection from all of the other animals.

One day Nanabosho was very hungry, so he started to fish. He wasn't having any luck catching fish anywhere.

All of a sudden, a little turtle poked his head out from under a rock near the stream and said: "Nanabosho, my brother, why don't you go down the stream to where the rocks are? There are lots of fish there."

"OK," said Nanabosho, "I'll try to fish over there."

After he went down to where the rocks were, he caught lots of fish. That evening he had a wonderful supper. With a full stomach, he went back to thank Turtle.

"Meegwetch, my little brother Turtle, I had a fantastic supper. Now I am going to do you a favour."

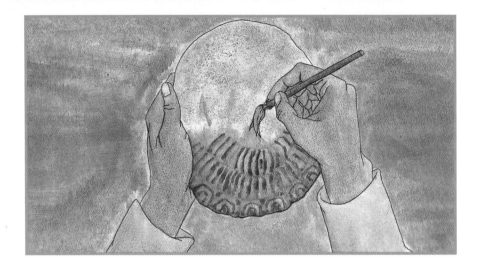

He looked around until he found a round rock. He picked it up and painted it beautiful colours.

He put it on top of Turtle and showed him how to pull his head, arms and legs inside.

"From now on this rock will be your shell. It will protect you from the other animals, as thanks for showing Nanabosho where to fish."

■ ■ ■

As we arrived back at Auntie Matrine's home, the story ended. We all asked for another one.

"It's time to get ready for bed now," said Nokomis, "tomorrow is another day and there will be another story."

AFTER YOU READ

Retell a story

In your own words, tell how the turtle got its shell.

The Paper Bag Princess

Written by Robert Munsch
Illustrated by Michael Martchenko

READING TIP

Think about what you know

Princesses are often in fairy tales. As you read, think about how this princess is the same as other princesses you've read about. How is she different?

Elizabeth was a beautiful princess. She lived in a castle and had expensive princess clothes. She was going to marry a prince named Ronald.

Unfortunately, a dragon smashed her castle, burned all her clothes with his fiery breath, and carried off Prince Ronald.

Elizabeth decided to chase the dragon and get Ronald back.

She looked everywhere for something to wear, but the only thing she could find that was not burnt was a paper bag. So she put on the paper bag and followed the dragon.

He was easy to follow, because he left a trail of burnt forests and horses' bones.

Finally, Elizabeth came to a cave with a large door that had a huge knocker on it. She took hold of the knocker and banged on the door.

The dragon stuck his nose out of the door and said, "Well, a princess! I love to eat princesses, but I have already eaten a whole castle today. I am a very busy dragon. Come back tomorrow."

He slammed the door so fast that Elizabeth almost got her nose caught.

Elizabeth grabbed the knocker and banged on the door again.

The dragon stuck his nose out of the door and said, "Go away. I love to eat princesses, but I have already eaten a whole castle today. I am a very busy dragon. Come back tomorrow."

"Wait," shouted Elizabeth. "Is it true that you are the smartest and fiercest dragon in the whole world?"

"Yes," said the dragon.

"Is it true," said Elizabeth, "that you can burn up ten forests with your fiery breath?"

"Oh, yes," said the dragon, and he took a huge, deep breath and breathed out so much fire that he burnt up fifty forests.

"Fantastic," said Elizabeth, and the dragon took another huge breath and breathed out so much fire that he burnt up one hundred forests.

"Magnificent," said Elizabeth, and the dragon took another huge breath, but this time nothing came out. The dragon didn't even have enough fire left to cook a meatball.

Elizabeth said, "Dragon, is it true that you can fly around the world in just ten seconds?"

"Why, yes," said the dragon, and jumped up and flew all the way around the world in just ten seconds.

He was very tired when he got back, but Elizabeth shouted, "Fantastic, do it again!"

So the dragon jumped up and flew around the whole world in just twenty seconds.

When he got back he was too tired to talk, and he lay down and went straight to sleep.

Elizabeth whispered, very softly, "Hey, dragon." The dragon didn't move at all.

She lifted up the dragon's ear and put her head right inside. She shouted as loud as she could, "Hey, dragon!"

The dragon was so tired he didn't even move.

Elizabeth walked right over the dragon and opened the door to the cave.

There was Prince Ronald. He looked at her and said, "Elizabeth, you are a mess! You smell like ashes, your hair is all tangled and you are wearing a dirty old paper bag. Come back when you are dressed like a real princess."

"Ronald," said Elizabeth, "your clothes are really pretty and your hair is very neat. You look like a real prince, but you are a bum."

They didn't get married after all.

AFTER YOU READ

Make a chart

Write two ways this princess is the same as other princesses. Write two ways she is different.

Same	Different

A Drum

Written by Susan Milord
Illustrated by Tadeusz Majewski

READING TIP

Read new words

When you come to a word you don't know, read on
to the end of the sentence. Then read the sentence
again thinking about what word would make sense.

There once was a poor widow who had only one
child, a son. He was a kindhearted boy, always
willing to help out in any way he could. As long as
he and his mother had each other, the boy didn't
mind that his clothing was ragged or that he had
only a few toys.

The boy had been secretly wishing for
something, however. He had always wanted a
drum. One day when his mother was going to the
village to sell some of their grain, she asked, "Is
there anything you would like from the market?"

The boy stopped, then said, "All I would really like, Mother, is a drum. I know you won't be able to get me one, but that is what I would really like."

The poor woman thought of her son all the way home from the market, saddened that she was not able to get him the one thing he really wanted. She bent down to pick up a piece of wood she saw lying by the side of the road. "Perhaps my good son can find a use for this," she thought. "It's not much, but at least it's something."

The boy didn't know what to do with the wood when his mother gave it to him, but he thanked her and carried it with him when he went out to play.

Down the road, the boy could see an old woman kneeling beside a cookstove. Her eyes were watering, and the boy asked her why she was crying. "I can't get my fire to burn," she replied.

"Here," said the boy, handing her his piece of wood. "Perhaps this will help." In no time at all, the old woman was able to get the fire going. She thanked the boy, giving him a *chapati* (chah–PAH–tee), a round, flat bread, that she cooked in a pan on the stove.

The boy took the bread and walked on until he met another woman, this one the wife of the village potter. She held a small child in her arms, but the child was crying. "Why is your child crying?" the boy asked.

The potter's wife answered. "Because he is hungry. We have nothing for him to eat." The boy looked at the chapati he was holding in his hand, then offered it to the unhappy child. The child nibbled at the bread and stopped crying at once.

By way of thanks, the grateful mother gave the boy a large pot.

The boy hadn't gone far when he came to the river, where he found a man and woman arguing. "What is the trouble?" asked the boy.

"I am a washerman," the man replied, "and my wife has just broken the only pot I had to boil clothes in. I'll never get the clothing clean now."

The boy knew that he had a solution to this man's problem, too, and gave the couple the pot he was carrying. "Thank you very much," the washerman said, and gave the boy a coat for his kindness.

The boy walked on further until he came to a man leading a horse along the road. His hair was wet, and he was shivering. The boy approached the man and asked, "What happened to your clothes, and why are you all wet?"

"I was on my way to visit relatives when a robber galloped up on this horse," the man replied. "He demanded I give him my clothes. Then he pushed me into the river."

The boy handed the man the coat he'd been given by the washerman. "Here," he said, "put this on." The man slipped on the garment. "Please take the horse," he told the boy. "The robber left it, and I have no need for it."

So the boy took the horse, and before long he came upon a wedding party. "Why do you all look so glum?" the boy asked.

The father of the bridegroom spoke up. "We are waiting for the man who is bringing the horse my son will ride. If he doesn't arrive soon we shall be late for the wedding."

The boy listened to this story, then offered the bridegroom his horse. "You have saved the day!" the groom exclaimed. Turning to speak with his father and one of the musicians, the groom handed the boy a drum. "Please accept one of our drums, with all of our thanks."

The boy's face lit up with joy. "Oh, thank you," he cried. "And much happiness to you on your wedding day!"

The boy ran all the way home, as fast as his feet would take him. His mother stared at the drum in disbelief as her son told her the story of how he had come to own it, starting with the piece of wood she had picked up along the side of the road.

AFTER YOU READ

Make a list

Write three new words you learned in the story. How did you figure out what they mean?

Stories Alive

You have read different kinds of stories. Now it's your turn to share one of your favourite stories. You can give a book talk.

Plan

- Choose a story or a book you like.

> **Idea!**
>
> Choose a book you think that other children might like, too!

- Tell important information about your story
  - ▶ What kind of story or book is it?
  - ▶ Who is the author?
  - ▶ Who are the main characters?
  - ▶ What is the story problem?
  - ▶ Why do you like the story?

> If you like stories about horses, you'll love this book.

- Find a good part to read aloud. Remember to choose a part that will make others want to read the story. But don't give the whole story away!
- Show the book to your audience.
- Finish by saying who might like to read the story.

Revise

Practise your book talk.
- Does it make sense?
- Have you used words like "because" to show how your ideas fit together?
- Can you add more interesting parts?

Ask a family member to listen to you practise.

Check

Listen to yourself on a tape recorder.
- Do you speak clearly?
- Is there expression in your voice?

Share

You could share your book talk with the class or a group of friends.

Remember:
Be ready to answer questions about the book.

ACKNOWLEDGMENTS

Permission to reprint copyrighted material is gratefully acknowledged. Every effort has been made to trace ownership of all copyrighted material and to secure permission from copyright holders. In the event of any question arising as to the use of any material, we will be pleased to make the necessary corrections in future printings.

"Whoa!" from *If You Could Wear My Sneakers!* by Sheree Fitch © 1997 (poetry) and Darcia Labrosse © 1997 (illustrations). Reproduced by permission of Doubleday Canada. Mama, Do You Love Me? text copyright © 1991 by Barbara M. Joose. Illustrations copyright © 1991 by Barbara Lavallee. All rights reserved. Used with permission of Chronicle Books. "Left Behind" text and selected illustrations from LEFT BEHIND by Carol Carrick. Text copyright © 1988 by Carol Carrick. Illustrations copyright © 1988 by Donald Carrick. Reprinted by permission of Clarion Books/Houghton Mifflin Co. All rights reserved. "Ladder to the Sky" taken from Toes in My Nose and Other Poems by Sheree Fitch and illustrated by Molly Bobak © 1987. Reproduced with permission of Doubleday Canada Limited. "New World" from Falling Up by Shel Silverstein. Copyright © 1996 by Shel Silverstein. Reproduced with permission of HarperCollins Publishers. "Running" from IT'S RAINING LAUGHTER by Nikki Grimes. Copyright © 1997 by Nikki Grimes. Used by permission of Dial Books for Young Readers, a division of Penguin Putnam Inc. The Crane Girl, text and illustrations © Veronika Martenova Charles, 1992. Reprinted with permission of Stoddart Publishing Co. Limited, Don Mills, Ont. "My Wish for Tomorrow" Selections used from *My Wish for Tomorrow*. A collaboration between Jim Henson Publishing and the United Nations. Copyright © 1995 United Nations. All rights reserved. Used by permission of Tambourine Books, a division of William Morrow & Co., Inc. A Salmon for Simon, text copyright © 1978 by Betty Waterton, illustrations copyright © 1978 by Ann Blades. A Groundwood Book/Douglas & McIntyre. "Information Detectives" by Susan Green © 1999 ITP Nelson. "Water, Water Everywhere" excerpt from Water, Water Everywhere by Melvin and Gilda Berger. Text copyright © 1995 by Melvin and Gilda Berger. Used by permission of Hambleton-Hill Publishing Inc. "How to Make a Water Magnifier" material from Have Fun with Magnifying by the Ontario Science Centre. Used by permission of Kids Can Press Ltd., Toronto. Text copyright © 1987 by The Centennial Centre of Science and Technology. "The Penny Experiment" abridged from Experiment with Water by Bryan Murphy. Used with permission of Two Can Publishing Ltd. "Washing the Willow Tree Loon" reprinted with the permission of Simon & Schuster Books for Young Readers, an imprint of Simon & Schuster Children's Publishing Division from Washing the Willow Tree Loon by Jacqueline Briggs Martin. Text copyright © 1995 Jacqueline Briggs Martin. Nanabosho: How the Turtle Got Its Shell by Joe McLellan. Winnipeg: Pemmican Publications Inc., 1994. Reprinted by permission. The Paper Bag Princess - story by Robert N. Munsch; illustrations by Michael Martchenko. © 1980 Bob Munsch Enterprises Ltd. (text); © 1980 Michael Martchenko (art). Reproduced with permission of Annick Press Ltd. "A Drum" from Tales Alive! By Susan Milord. Copyright © 1995 by Susan Milord. Reproduced with permission of Williamson Publishing.

Illustrations
Cover: Amy Wummer; pp. 6-7 Joe Weissmann; pp. 8-13 Barbara Lavallee; pp. 14-23 Donald Carrick; p. 25 Kevin Hawkes; p. 27 Shel Silverstein; pp. 28-37 Veronika Martenova Charles; p. 38 (top) Jean Tan, (bottom) Sofia Abrantes; p. 39 (left) Yuriko Tanaka, (right) Lo Min Ming; p. 40 (top) Ho Pei Rong, (bottom) Nery Briones Padilla; p. 41 (top) Mayra Garra Galma, (bottom) Samantha Louise Eddie; pp. 42-55 Ann Blades; pp. 56-57, 71 Tina Holdcroft; pp. 74-81 Bart Vallecoccia; pp. 82-87 Blanche Sims; p. 88 Allan Moon; pp. 90-101 Stephen Marchesi; p. 102 Tina Holdcroft; pp. 104-105 Jenny Campbell; pp. 106-111 Rhian Brynjolson; pp. 112-119 Michael Martchenko; pp. 120-125 Tadeusz Majewski; 126-127 Tina Holdcroft

Photographs
p. 26 © Myles C. Pinkey; pp. 58-66, 68-69 Dave Starrett; p. 72 (top) © Darrell Gulin/Tony Stone Images, (bottom) © PhotoDisc, Inc; p.73 (top left) © Paul Morrell/ Tony Stone Images, (bottom left) © Gerben Oppermans/Tony Stone Images, (right) © PhotoDisc, Inc; p. 88 Dave Starrett